FAST FACTS

Fantastic Mammals

KINGFISHER

NEW YORK

Copyright © Macmillan Publishers International Ltd 2016
Published in the United States by Kingfisher,
175 Fifth Ave., New York, NY 10010
Kingfisher is an imprint of Macmillan Children's Books, London
All rights reserved.

Distributed in the U.S. and Canada by Macmillan,
175 Fifth Ave., New York, NY 10010

Library of Congress Cataloging-in-Publication data
has been applied for.

Interior design by Tall Tree Ltd
Cover design by Peter Clayman

Adapted from an original text by David Burnie
Literacy consultants: Kerenza Ghosh, Stephanie Laird

ISBN 978-0-7534-7274-3 (HB)
ISBN 978-0-7534-7275-0 (PB)

Kingfisher books are available for special promotions
and premiums. For details contact: Special Markets
Department, Macmillan, 175 Fifth Ave.,
New York, NY 10010.

For more information, please visit
www.kingfisherbooks.com

Printed in China

9 8 7 6 5 4 3 2 1
1TR/0116/WKT/UG/128MA

Picture credits
The Publisher would like to thank the following for permission to reproduce their material.
Top = t; Bottom = b; Center = c; Left = l; Right = r
Front cover Shutterstock/Donovan van Staden; Back cover iStock/Craig Dingle; Pages 1 Shutterstock/Kersti
Joergensen; 3 FLPA/Thomas Mangelson/Minden; 4cr Shutterstock/Vladimir Melnik; 4cl Shutterstock/Mogens
Trolle; 4c Shutterstock/Joy Brown; 4br Shutterstock/Eric Isselee; 4–5t Naturepl/Brendon Cole; 4–5b Shutterstock/
Susan Flashman; 5tr Frank Lane Picture Agency (FLPA)/Hugh Lansdown; 5c Shutterstock/Sharon Morris;
5r Shutterstock/Milena; 5bl Ardea/John Daniels; 5br Naturepl/Anup Shah; 6-7 Polygone Studios; 6c Getty/Steve
Bloom; 7t Shutterstock/Susan Flashman; 7r Getty/Steve Bloom; 8c Shutterstock/MikeE; 9tr Photoshot/Nigel J
Dennis/NHPA; 9cr Photoshot/Nigel J Dennis/NHPA; 9br Photoshot/Nigel J Dennis/NHPA; 10bl Alamy/
WorldFoto; 10–11 Shutterstock/Pichugin Dmitry; 11cr Alamy/agefotostock; 12t Alamy/Eclectic Images;
12 Alamy/Gallo Images and Shutterstock/neelsky and Shutterstock/David Young; 12–13 Shutterstock/EcoPrint;
13c FLPA/Vincent Grafhorst/Minden; 14c Shutterstock/palko72; 14b Shutterstock/EcoPrint; 15tr Shutterstock/
topten22photo; 15brl Shutterstock/Olga Selyutina; 15brc Shutterstock/Jeff Banke; 15brr Shutterstock/Jakub
Krechowicz; 16tl Shutterstock/worldswildlifewonders; 16c FLPA/Nobert Wu/Minden; 17t FLPA/Flip Nicklin/
Minden; 17c Shutterstock/A J Gallant; 17cr Seapics/Richard Herrmann; 17b FLPA/Flip Nicklin/Minden;
20tl Alamy/John Warburton-Lee; 20lct Shutterstock/worldswildlifewonders; 20lcb Alamy/Imagebroker;
20b Shutterstock/Eric Isselee; 20tr Alamy/Wolfgang Kaehler; 21tl Shutterstock/livestockimages;
21b Shutterstock/Sharon Morris; 22tc Shutterstock/javarman; 22bl Shutterstock/Timothy Craig Lubcke;
23c Shutterstock/Kersti Joergensen; 23tr FLPA/Konrad Wothe/Mindenl; 24–25 FLPA/Thomas Mangelson/Minden;
24bl Shutterstock/Scenic Shutterbug; 28tl Press Association/AP; 29cr Corbis/Olah Tibor/epa; 29b Alamy/Images
of Africa.

Contents

Mammals are amazing

The first mammals lived side by side with the dinosaurs, more than 200 million years ago. The dinosaurs died out but mammals survived. Mammals are warm-blooded, they have hair or fur, and they raise their young on milk.

Keeping warm

Most mammals are covered with fur, which helps keep their body warm. Mammals that swim often have a layer of fat just under their skin instead. The fat layer of a walrus can be six inches (15 centimeters) thick.

Along with okapis, giraffes make up a small family of African mammals. They have a long neck and a long tongue.

The elephant family includes three species —two from Africa and one from Asia.

Anteaters have a long snout without any teeth. They live on the ground or in trees.

We are family

Scientists divide mammals into about 150 different families. The mammals in some families, called **marsupials**, raise their young in a pouch. In other mammals, called placentals, the young develop inside the mother's body until birth. Placentals include humans, cats, and blue whales.

Orcas, or killer whales, have pointed teeth and hunt large **prey**.

warm-blooded
Having a body temperature that stays warm and steady, whatever the conditions outside.

Unlike most other bats, fruit bats are vegetarians, tracking down fruit by its color and smell.

Zebras belong to a large family of plant-eating mammals with a hard hoof on each foot.

The gray kangaroo is one of the largest marsupials. It can bound at speeds of up to 30 mph (50 km/h).

Brown rats are rodents—mammals with **gnawing** teeth.

Tigers belong to the cat family. Like most cats, they hunt on their own, and feed entirely on meat.

Most lemurs live in trees, but the ring-tailed lemur spends a lot of its life on the ground.

Clinging on

The nocturnal flying lemur, or colugo, is a placental mammal that lives in the Philippine rain forest. It gives birth to tiny young after a pregnancy of just 60 days. The baby clings to its mother's belly for the first six months. When not gliding, the mother wraps her gliding **membrane** around her baby to protect it and keep it warm.

A flying lemur weighs only about 1.2 ounces (35 grams) at birth.

The Philippine flying lemur can glide up to 330 feet (100 meters).

Water birth

A female hippopotamus usually gives birth underwater, pushing the newly born calf to the surface so it can breathe. She stays in the water without eating for several days, only leaving to graze when the baby is strong enough. Baby hippos drink their mother's milk for up to eight months.

The membrane reaches from neck to tip of tail.

Starting life

There are two kinds of mammal that lay eggs. All other mammals give birth to live young. The young of placental mammals, including humans, develop inside their mother's womb before being born. Marsupials, including kangaroos, give birth to young at a very early stage and the babies grow in a protective pouch.

Mammal eggs

The short-nosed echidna (spiny anteater) is a monotreme. The female develops a backward-facing pouch on her underside and lays a single leathery egg in it. The baby echidna, or puggle, feeds from a special patch on her skin that oozes milk.

Echidnas live in Australia and New Guinea.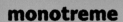

monotreme
An egg-laying mammal. Echidnas and platypuses are monotremes.

A long first journey

When a baby kangaroo, or joey, is born, it is only about one inch (two centimeters) long. The marsupial has to haul itself all the way up its mother's body and into a pouch, where there are four teats. It attaches itself to a teat and feeds on its mother's milk. There may be more joeys of different ages in the pouch at the same time.

The joey will leave the pouch completely by the time it is 10 months old.

The baby takes 2–3 years to reach adult size.

The baby clings to mother's belly as she glides.

TOP FIVE BITESIZE FACTS

- An elephant's pregnancy lasts for 22 months.

- Naked mole rats can give birth to as many as 25 young in one litter.

- After giving birth, a whale mother pushes her newborn calf straight to the surface of the water to take its first breath.

- All baby mammals drink their mother's milk.

- A joey's journey to its mother's pouch takes up to five minutes after it has been born.

Defense

At the first sign of trouble, most mammals try to make an emergency escape, but a small number use special defenses to hold their ground. They include pangolins, which have built-in armor plating, and porcupines, which are protected by hundreds of sharp quills.

Two against one

With its back facing danger, an African porcupine tries to fend off two hungry lions. The lions are intent on flipping it over, so they can reach its furry underside. Each time they move closer, the porcupine rattles its quills and reverses. The quills can detach easily, embedding themselves in a lion's skin.

quills
Extra-large hairs with sharp points that an animal uses to defend itself.

TOP FIVE BITESIZE FACTS

- An African porcupine's quills can be 12 inches (30 centimeters) long.

- Porcupines give off a strong smell when they raise their quills as a warning to **predators**.

- Skunks defend themselves by squirting a foul-smelling liquid at attackers.

- Porcupines can have up to 30,000 quills.

- A pangolin's scales are tough and sharp. It can defend itself by using its tail as a jagged club.

If quills get stuck in the skin, they remain embedded and can cause fatal wounds.

An African porcupine's quills have backward-facing barbs that catch on skin and make them hard to pull out.

Armor plating

Millions of years ago, giant, armored mammals roamed Earth. Some were as big as cars. These giants eventually died out, but armored mammals still exist today—including armadillos, which are covered in bony plates, and pangolins, which have overlapping scales. Some species roll up to protect soft body parts inside.

Pangolin stops and tucks in its head when threatened.

Legs disappear beneath the pangolin's sharp-edged scales.

Tail curls up, hiding the legs and head, forming a protective ball shape.

In extreme places

Mammals live in some of the hottest, coldest, highest, and driest places on Earth. They have special physical features that help them survive. These include amazingly warm fur, thick layers of body fat, and the ability to take all their water from their food.

Cells in the hump store fat – a substance that provides energy when food is hard to find.

Double protection

Bactrian camels live in Central Asia, where it is hot in summer and freezing in winter, and dry nearly all the time. They store fat in their two humps, and they keep warm with a long winter coat, which falls off in large patches during spring.

habitat: deserts of Central Asia, from Mongolia to China

High life

Vicuñas live at altitudes as high as 18,000 feet (5500 meters), where the oxygen in the air is extremely thin. Here, human hikers soon get tired, but vicuñas can run up steep slopes with ease. Their secret: special red blood **cells** that get the most oxygen from every breath.

habitat: Andes mountains, from Peru to Chile

insulating
Helps keep an animal's body from becoming too warm or too cold.

TOP FIVE BITESIZE FACTS

- In the Arctic of northern Canada, some ground squirrels **hibernate** for nine months each year.

- Polar bears have little bumps on the pads of their paws for good grip on ice.

- Camels can go for up to six days without drinking water in summer, and up to six months in winter.

- During winter, Bactrian camels eat snow to quench their thirst.

- The fennec fox keeps cool by losing heat through its enormous ears.

A camel's undercoat is made of fine hairs that trap air, creating an insulating layer that keeps its body warm.

habitat: northern Arctic, in North America, Europe and Asia

Winter wrap
The Arctic fox is one of the world's most coldproof mammals, thanks to its exceptionally thick winter fur. It can survive in temperatures as low as –58 °F (–50 °C), using its bushy tail to protect its feet and face from the icy wind. In spring, its white winter coat is replaced by a much thinner one, colored brownish-gray.

Calls and signals

All mammals have to communicate, even if they spend most of their life on their own. Meerkats live in groups, or packs, and they use special calls to warn of danger as they search for food. Like most mammals, meerkats also leave signals in their scent. These help mark **territory** around their **burrows**.

Martial eagles often weigh five times as much as meerkats, and can carry them off in their claws.

An alarm signal for an eagle is a drawn-out call. When sounded, the entire meerkat pack vanishes underground.

The inner lining of the snout is full of nerves. These are sensitive to smells and scent signals, or pheromones.

pheromone

A smell, often working in tiny amounts, that animals use to communicate.

Intruder alert

Sentries watch out for danger, and they also sniff the air for meerkats from other groups, which have an unfamiliar smell. Young male meerkats often move to new packs, searching for a chance to **breed**. Sentries will sometimes let them in, but often the pack fights them off.

On the alert

Meerkats live in dry parts of southwest Africa, where they feed on insects and other small animals. They set off in a group, keeping in touch with soft, twittering noises as they fan out over the ground. While most of the pack is busy feeding, sentries stand up on their back legs. They watch and listen, sounding the alarm if any predators or intruders head their way.

Propped up by its tail, a sentry can keep watch for danger for up to an hour.

Adult cobras are dangerous enemies, particularly if they get into the pack's burrows.

Scent signals

Meerkats leave scent signals around their burrows by rubbing their body against a rock or tree. Pack leaders will also "scent mark" junior members to remind them who's in charge and to show that they belong to the pack.

Unique mammals

No other mammals look like elephants or share their way of life. Weighing up to seven tons each, elephants are the biggest land animals and the last survivors in a family that once included **mammoths** from the last **Ice Age**. Today, there are three species of these huge animals.

Leading by example

Elephant **herds** are based around females and their young. Each herd is led by a senior female, or matriarch, who leads the herd to food or water, following paths that she has memorized over many years. Female calves stay in the herd, but males leave it in their early teens. They live in small groups, meeting females only when they mate. Female African elephants are ready to breed by the age of ten.

Huge cheek teeth grind up food. There are 24, but only four work at a time. Worn-out teeth move forward and then drop out.

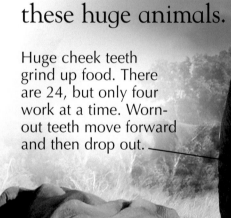

Enormous ears are used to signal mood and to control body temperature.

Tusks are giant **incisor** teeth that grow through an elephant's upper jaw. They are made mainly of ivory.

Working elephants

African elephants are hard to tame, but Asian elephants have been kept in captivity for thousands of years. They are still used for ceremonial purposes, but now they are becoming rare in the wild.

This decorated elephant is carrying people during a religious ceremony in Thailand.

TOP FIVE BITESIZE FACTS

- 🐾 The biggest known tusks from an African elephant are just under 12 feet (3.5 meters) long.

- 🐾 In Uganda, forest elephants march deep into caves to feed on salt deposits.

- 🐾 An elephant's trunk contains more than 40,000 muscles.

- 🐾 A trunk can lift more than 660 pounds (300 kilograms).

- 🐾 Elephants have a better sense of smell than any other mammal.

ivory
A hard substance found in the tusks of mammals such as elephants, walruses, and hippos.

The trunk can suck up water or dust without it getting into the elephant's lungs.

Types of elephant

The savanna elephant and forest elephant both live in Africa. They have gigantic ears and trunks with two flexible tips. The Asian elephant is smaller, and has a single tip on its trunk.

Asian   forest   savanna

In the water

Most mammals can swim, even though they normally live on dry land. But some are truly at home in water. Sea lions and sea otters dive for food among forests of giant kelp (seaweed), while elephant seals plunge into the ocean depths to catch their prey.

A sea lion has six long front teeth for gripping its slippery prey.

Clash of the giants

Named after their inflatable trunk, male elephant seals can weigh up to three tons. During the breeding season they fight for supremacy, rearing up and stabbing with their teeth. After walruses, elephant seals are the largest seals, or pinnipeds.

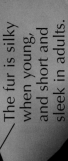

The fur is silky when young, and short and sleek in adults.

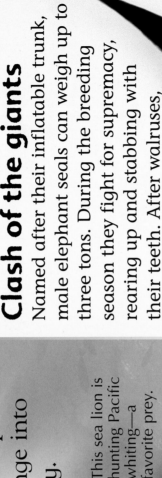

This sea lion is hunting Pacific whiting—a favorite prey.

Hunters in the kelp

The California sea lion is lean, agile, and intelligent, with a streamlined body. To swim, it uses its front flippers to propel itself forward and its hind ones to steer. On land, it bounds along on all four flippers. True seals, also known as phocids, are more clumsy on the shore. They shuffle along on their stomach, with their flippers by their sides.

Offshore otter

The sea otter is the only otter species that lives almost entirely offshore. Diving down into the kelp, it uses its paws to collect small sea animals, carefully avoiding their pincers and spines.

Instead of eating on the spot, it carries food to the surface, often tucking it into a fold of skin.

Sea otters have the world's densest fur. The hairs trap a layer of air, keeping the skin dry.

The front flippers have the same bones as a human arm and hand, although in different sizes. A web of leathery skin forms the flipper's blade.

TOP FIVE BITESIZE FACTS

🐾 Seals and sea lions have to come onto land to breed.

🐾 Elephant seals can dive up to one mile (1.5 kilometers) deep and hold their breath for more than an hour.

🐾 Dugongs and manatees are diving mammals that graze on seagrass.

🐾 Lying on their back on the ocean surface, sea otters hold hands to stop them from drifting apart.

🐾 A sea otter's fur has one million hairs per square inch (150,000 per square centimeter), the same number as on the whole of a human head.

A sea otter hunts crabs.

pinniped
A meat-eating mammal with flippers and a streamlined body.

The sperm whale's large fluke drives it forward.

Measuring up to 90 feet (27 meters) long, the blue whale is by far the world's biggest animal.

Family group

Whales, dolphins, and porpoises belong to a single family of mammals, called the cetaceans. There are about 80 different kinds, from the mighty blue whale to the tiny vaquita, which is smaller than most seals. Cetaceans have blowholes on top of their head, which close up when they dive.

blowhole
The nostril of a whale or dolphin, which allows the animal to breathe while staying almost submerged.

Ocean giants

The sperm whale's huge head is filled with waxy oil, which adjusts its buoyancy during dives. Sperm whales feed on giant squid at up to 9840 feet (3000 meters) deep.

Roaming the oceans, whales and dolphins spend their whole lives at sea. They have a streamlined body, two front flippers, and a horizontal **fluke**, or tail. Most have teeth, but the largest whales are toothless. They filter small animals from the water, using a mouth that works like a giant sieve.

A sperm whale's lower jaw has up to 28 pairs of sharply pointed teeth. Each tooth is up to 8 inches (20 centimeters) long—bigger than any other predator's.

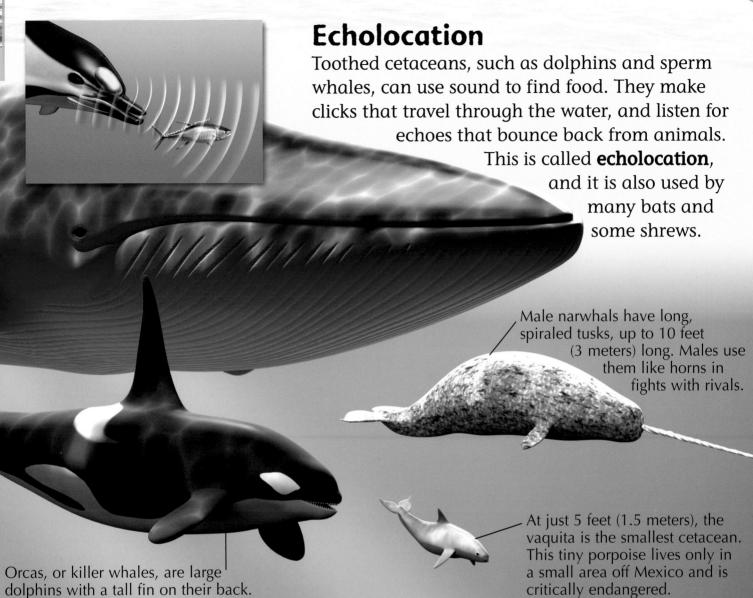

Echolocation

Toothed cetaceans, such as dolphins and sperm whales, can use sound to find food. They make clicks that travel through the water, and listen for echoes that bounce back from animals. This is called **echolocation**, and it is also used by many bats and some shrews.

Male narwhals have long, spiraled tusks, up to 10 feet (3 meters) long. Males use them like horns in fights with rivals.

At just 5 feet (1.5 meters), the vaquita is the smallest cetacean. This tiny porpoise lives only in a small area off Mexico and is critically endangered.

Orcas, or killer whales, are large dolphins with a tall fin on their back. They live in groups, eating seals, sharks, and sometimes other whales.

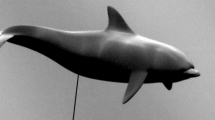

Found worldwide, except near the poles, the bottlenose dolphin is fast, acrobatic, and smart. It lives in small groups, or pods, and eats fish and squid.

TOP FIVE BITESIZE FACTS

🐾 The Amazon river dolphin is nearly blind. It catches fish and turtles using echolocation.

🐾 A blue whale's heart is the size of a small car.

🐾 Male humpback whales sing songs that other whales can hear hundreds of miles away.

🐾 A dolphin can jump twenty feet (six meters) out of the water.

🐾 A blue whale calf can drink 880 pints (500 liters) of milk per day.

The guereza is a leaf-eating monkey from Central and East Africa. It is white when it is born, but gradually changes color to black and white.

Agile and intelligent, vervet monkeys are a common sight in East and southern Africa. They often come down to the ground, and steal food in towns and on farmland.

Like all lemurs, the indri is found only in Madagascar. It leaps from tree to tree with its body upright, and its arms and legs open wide.

Woolly spider monkeys, or muriquis, can feed by hanging on with their tail. They live in Brazil's Atlantic forest—a threatened habitat that has almost disappeared.

prehensile
Describes a body part that is able to wrap tightly around something and hang on.

Meet the primates

With grasping hands and forward-facing eyes, primates are smart mammals that often have a large brain for their size. Some primates are expert problem-solvers and can make and use tools. We humans are primates ourselves and intelligence is one of the secrets of our success.

Primates of the world

There are about 250 types of primate. Most live in tropical forests and, although some are vegetarians, many eat a wide range of food, from leaves and fruit to insects and eggs. Primates have long arms and legs, with flexible fingers and toes, and many also have a prehensile tail that can hold all their weight. Eyes that face forward make primates good at judging distances. This is a vital skill when leaping from branch to branch.

Tarsiers, from Southeast Asia, are tiny primates that hunt insects at night. They watch for prey using their giant eyes, and then leap toward it through the dark.

Africa's gorillas are the world's largest primates, weighing up to 440 pounds (200 kilograms). Despite their size and strength, they are harmless vegetarians, spending most of their time on the ground.

TOP FIVE BITESIZE FACTS

🐾 The smallest primate is the mouse lemur. It is just 4 inches (10 centimeters) long.

🐾 Japanese macaques keep warm during winter by bathing in hot springs.

🐾 Chimpanzees and bonobos are the closest animal relatives of humans.

🐾 Chimps often grin when they are afraid or nervous.

🐾 Monkeys in Central and South America have prehensile tails, but monkeys that live elsewhere do not.

21

Smart orangutans

An orangutan swings through the trees.

Orangutans are apes that feed mainly on fruit and spend almost all of their lives in trees. They usually live alone, although youngsters stay with their mother for eight years—one of the longest childhoods in the animal world. They are smart, quick to learn and, despite their size, surprisingly agile.

Young orangutans have light, delicate fur, but adults have coarse fur that is downward-trailing to help shed the rain. Orangutan fur color varies from orange to rusty red.

Holding tight

Orangutans are born with a strong grip, and they use it every minute of their life. Babies cling to their mother's fur, while adults clamber along branches with their leathery hands and feet. As orangutans are heavy, they can make slender trees sway under their weight. When a tree bends down, an orangutan steps off it and grabs one nearby—an efficient way of traveling above the forest floor.

Face flaps

Male orangutans can be twice as heavy as females. As the male matures, he develops wide cheek flaps to show he is **dominant** over other males. Male orangutans breed from the age of 15 but, unlike females, play no part in looking after the young.

Orangutans eat more than 100 different types of fruit.

Unlike humans, orangutans have opposable big toes. This allows their feet to work like a second set of hands, clinging to branches.

apes
A group of tailless primates that includes chimpanzees, gorillas, orangutans, and humans.

Nesting time
Orangutans spend the night in temporary nests, which they build high up in trees. During the day, they roam through the forest, collecting most of their food in the treetops.

TOP FIVE BITESIZE FACTS

🐾 There are two species of orangutan—one species lives in Sumatra, the other in Borneo.

🐾 Orangutans collect insects and honey with specially prepared sticks.

🐾 The name "orangutan" means "person of the forest" in the Malay language.

🐾 Orangutans use giant leaves as umbrellas.

🐾 Only around 6000 Sumatran orangutans are left in the wild.

Hunters on land

With their massive body and powerful jaws, bears are some of the biggest land predators on the planet. The brown bear weighs nearly half a ton, with enough strength to kill a horse. Despite their size, most bears are omnivores, eating all kinds of food. Their menu ranges from fruit and seeds to fish, and even moths.

Bears have average eyesight, but their sense of smell is among the best of all mammals.

Brown bears have impressive incisors but, unlike most **carnivores**, their rear teeth are shaped for crushing plant food, instead of slicing up meat.

omnivore
An animal that eats all kinds of food, including meat and plants.

Winter birth

Many bears give birth in winter, which they spend tucked away inside dens. At first, the young are tiny, but they grow fast on their mother's milk. This female black bear has produced two cubs, which will leave her when they are 18 months old.

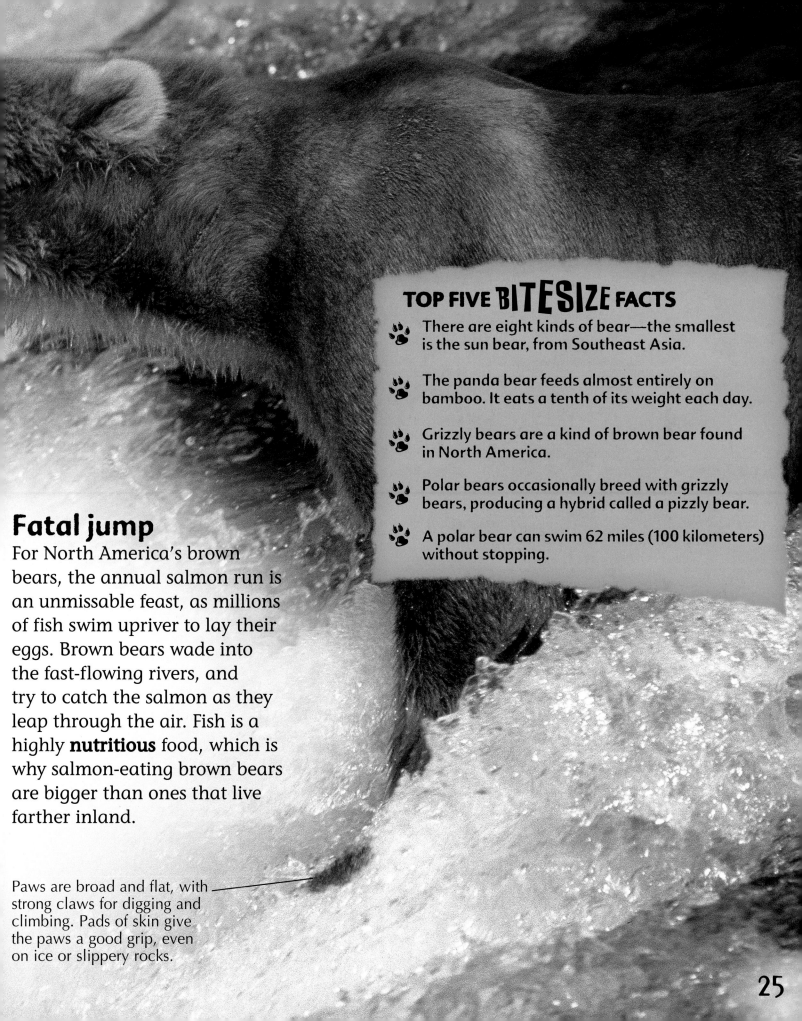

TOP FIVE BITESIZE FACTS

- 🐾 There are eight kinds of bear—the smallest is the sun bear, from Southeast Asia.

- 🐾 The panda bear feeds almost entirely on bamboo. It eats a tenth of its weight each day.

- 🐾 Grizzly bears are a kind of brown bear found in North America.

- 🐾 Polar bears occasionally breed with grizzly bears, producing a hybrid called a pizzly bear.

- 🐾 A polar bear can swim 62 miles (100 kilometers) without stopping.

Fatal jump

For North America's brown bears, the annual salmon run is an unmissable feast, as millions of fish swim upriver to lay their eggs. Brown bears wade into the fast-flowing rivers, and try to catch the salmon as they leap through the air. Fish is a highly **nutritious** food, which is why salmon-eating brown bears are bigger than ones that live farther inland.

Paws are broad and flat, with strong claws for digging and climbing. Pads of skin give the paws a good grip, even on ice or slippery rocks.

Gliders and fliers

When darkness falls, some mammals take to the air. Gliding mammals launch themselves from trees. Most gliders travel short distances, buoyed by flaps of elastic skin. Bats have real wings, made of leathery skin. They can stay airborne for hours.

To launch, the glider kicks itself off a tree.

The flight membrane has a thick edge.

Large eyes work well in dim light.

To land, the glider's body is steeply angled.

A gliding membrane connects the front and back legs. When not in use, it tightens up along the glider's sides.

Controlled descent

With skin flaps spread wide, the Australian sugar glider moves quickly and silently among the trees. It can travel more than 165 feet (50 meters) in a single jump, controlling its glide by angling its body and steering with its tail. The sugar glider is a marsupial, but this way of moving is also used by some other mammals, including some rodents and colugos, or flying lemurs.

Powered flight

Bats are the only mammals with wings, and the only ones that use their own muscle power to stay in the air. Predatory kinds, or microbats, are extremely agile fliers. They find their prey by echolocation—the same system used by dolphins and whales.

The leaf-nosed bat emits pulses of **ultrasound** from its strangely shaped "nose-leaf." Large ears detect echoes that bounce off obstacles and flying insects.

The wing membrane is stretched by thin and flexible finger bones, which flick as the wing beats. This helps the bat to zigzag through the air.

The flight membrane connects tail and legs.

flying insect prey found through echolocation

thin layer of double-sided skin

TOP FIVE BITESIZE FACTS

🐾 The smallest gliding mammal is the Australian feather-tailed glider.

🐾 There are 44 species of flying squirrel.

🐾 The largest bat in the world, the giant golden-crowned flying fox, has a wingspan of up to 5.6 feet (1.7 meters).

🐾 Fish-eating bats sense ripples on the surface of the water made by fish.

🐾 Vampire bats are the only mammals that feed entirely on blood, preying on livestock and birds.

microbat
A small or medium-sized bat that hunts insects or other animals.

Whale wars

There has been a ban on hunting whales since 1986, but some hunting continues. In 2007, these inflatable whales in Sydney, Australia, were used as a protest against a decision by Japan to resume hunting.

The danger list

A helicopter arrives to move the white rhino.

Many mammals are threatened by disappearing forests, hunting, pollution, and climate change. The danger list includes some of the world's best-known creatures which are at risk of extinction, such as tigers, rhinos, and giant pandas.

This rhino is being prepared for a helicopter airlift.

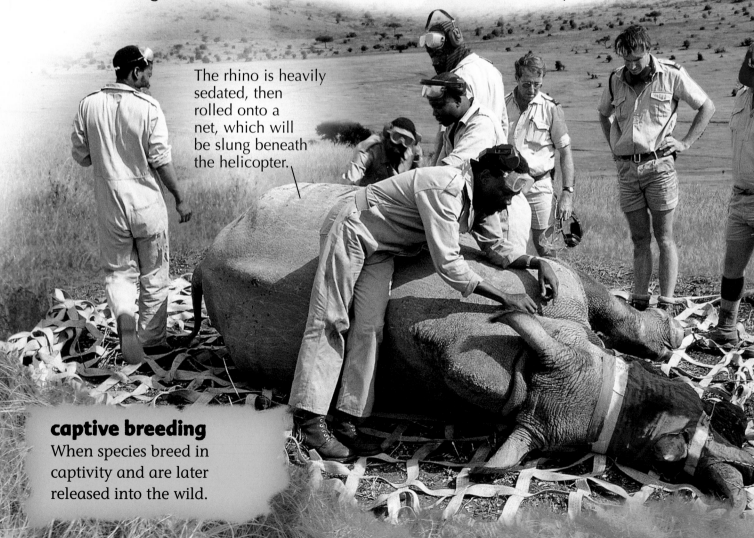

The rhino is heavily sedated, then rolled onto a net, which will be slung beneath the helicopter.

captive breeding
When species breed in captivity and are later released into the wild.

Airlift

With nearly 20,000 in game parks and sanctuaries, the southern white rhino is off the danger list, but its survival depends on around-the-clock conservation. The main threat comes from poachers, who target white rhinos for their horns, one of which can sell for thousands of dollars. Rhinos are looked after by teams of game wardens. Some rhinos are even flown by helicopter to new areas to reintroduce the species to places where they once thrived.

Ear notching is a quick and relatively painless way of identifying a rhino.

Back from the edge

Przewalski's horses from Mongolia are the only truly wild horses in the world. They were saved from extinction in the 20th century through captive breeding. About 300 now live in the wild.

Caught on camera

On the island of Borneo, a rare Sundaland clouded leopard triggers off an automatic camera. This kind of equipment is making it easier to keep track of endangered species. This is particularly true in forests and the deep ocean, where it is easy for animals to stay hidden.

Glossary

breed
To have offspring. Before mammals can breed, parents have to pair up and mate.

burrow
A home that is dug out underground. Most mammals dig their own burrows, using their feet or their teeth.

carnivore
Any animal that eats meat. In mammals, the same word is also used for the family that includes cats, dogs, wolves, and their relatives.

cell
Cells are the very tiny units that make up all living things. A mammal's body contains more than 200 types of cell.

dominant
Describes a high-ranking animal within a group. In lions, wolves, and many other mammals, only the dominant animals breed.

echolocation
Sensing food, or the way ahead, by making short bursts of sound and listening for echoes that come back.

fluke
The tail of a whale or dolphin. Unlike a fish's tail, flukes are horizontal, and move up and down to push the whale through the water. Flukes do not contain any hard struts or bones.

gnawing
Chewing using self-sharpening incisors, or front teeth.

herd
A group of mammals that stay together for most of their lives. Herds are usually made up of plant-eating mammals with hooves.

hibernate
Animals that hibernate go into a special kind of deep, winter sleep. It helps them survive cold weather, using food stored inside their bodies.

Ice Age
A long period of intense cold, causing glaciers and ice caps to expand. The last Ice Age ended about 10,000 years ago.

incisors
Flat-edged front teeth that mammals use to nip and to gnaw.

mammoth
A prehistoric member of the elephant family. Ice Age mammoths were often covered with long fur.

marsupial

A mammal that raises its young in a pouch. Most marsupials live in Australia and New Guinea, but some are found in North and South America.

membrane

A thin layer of living tissue, usually with its own blood supply and nerves.

nutritious

Full of nutrients—the substances that fuel an animal's body and let it grow.

prairie

A large area of open land where grasses, herbs, and shrubs grow rather than trees.

predator

An animal that hunts for its food.

prey

An animal that predators hunt for food.

rodent

A small or medium-sized mammal with front teeth that are specially shaped for gnawing.

species

A group of living things that look alike, and that breed only with their own kind.

streamlined

Having a smooth outline that slips easily through water or air.

territory

A piece of ground that an animal claims as its own, keeping rivals away. It usually contains enough food and space to raise a family.

ultrasound

Pulses of sound that are too high-pitched for human ears to hear. Bats, dolphins, and other mammals use ultrasound to find their food.

Index